PARTICIPANT'S EDITION

Celebrating an Authentic Passover Seder

A Haggadah for Home and Church

Joseph M. Stallings

Resource Publications, Inc.
San Jose, California

Editorial director: Kenneth Guentert
Prepress manager: Elizabeth J. Asborno

Reprint Department
Resource Publications, Inc.
160 E. Virginia Street #290
San Jose, CA 95112-5876

ISBN 0-89390-297-7

Printed in the United States of America

00 99 98 97 96 | 5 4 3 2 1

All Biblical and Talmudic translations are the author's.

Note: The pages in this Haggadah contain notes referring to the coinciding pages in Parts III and IV of *Celebrating an Authentic Passover Seder: A Haggadah for Home and Church* (Resource Publications, Inc., 1994).

HAGGADAH SHEL PESACH

THE PASSOVER SEDER

The Order

לְהַדְלִיק נֵר שֶׁל יוֹם טוֹב
Ner Shel Yom Tov
Lighting the Holy Day Lights

1.
קַדֵּשׁ
Kaddesh
Sanctifying the Feast

2.
וּרְחַץ
Urechatz
Washing of Hands

3.
כַּרְפַּס
Karpas
Eating the Greens

4.
יַחַץ
Yachatz
Breaking the Middle Matzah

5.
מַגִּיד
Maggid
Narrating the Exodus

6.
רָחְצָה
Rachatz
The Second Washing of Hands

7.
הַמּוֹצִיא
Ha-Motzi
The Breaking of Bread

of the Seder

8.
מַצָּה
Matzah
Reciting the Blessing

9.
מָרוֹר
Maror
Eating Bitter Herbs

10.
כּוֹרֵךְ
Korekh
Eating the Hillel Sandwich

11.
שֻׁלְחָן עוֹרֵךְ
Shulchan Orekh
Dinner Is Served

12.
צָפוּן
Tzafun
Returning the Afikoman

13.
בָּרֵךְ
Barekh
Giving Thanks for the Meal

14.
הַלֵּל
Hallel
Reciting the Hallel

15.
נִרְצָה
Nirtzah
Conclusion of the Seder

לְהַדְלִיק נֵר שֶׁל יוֹם טוֹב

Ner Shel Yom Tov

Lighting the Holy Day Lights

The evening celebration begins with the lighting of the festival candles by the women present.

The mother, wife, sister or daughter closest to the candle lights it.

All mothers, wives, sisters and daughters recite the following blessing:

We bless you O LORD our God,
the king of the universe
for you have sanctified us
through the observance of your commandments
and you have commanded us
to light these holy day lights.[1]

בָּרוּךְ אַתָּה יְיָ אֱלֹהֵנוּ
מֶלֶךְ הָעוֹלָם
אֲשֶׁר קִדְּשָׁנוּ
בְּמִצְוֹתָיו
וְצִוָּנוּ
לְהַדְלִק נֵר
שֶׁל יוֹם טוֹב

All Fathers and Mothers:

O LORD our God, bless our daughters as you blessed our spiritual mothers, Sarah and Rebecca, Rachel and Leah, and bless our sons as you blessed our spiritual fathers, Abraham and Isaac and Jacob, whom you blessed as Israel.

May God bless you and keep all of you.
May God be pleased with you and be gracious to you.
May God watch over all of you and grant you His peace! (Priestly Prayer, Num 6:25-27).

The Meaning of Passover Observance

Father:

Welcome to our seder.

Tonight we are participating in history's most ancient and continuously observed festival. Tonight's ritual is called a "seder" because it follows a prescribed order in the unfolding of the service. The word "seder" means "order" in Hebrew. Throughout this ritual we will celebrate two principal events in the history of God's people. We will participate in the Exodus from Egypt, and we will recall that Jesus observed Passover with his disciples on the night before he died.

Mother:

Our table is set for a festive meal. In reality, however, our table setting becomes an environment in which the events of the Exodus from Egypt will be relived by all of us. We read in the Mishnah[2] (the written deposit of the Oral Torah) that in every generation each person should think of herself or himself as personally coming forth out of Egypt. That is what the bible means when it says in Exodus 13:8, "And you shall explain to your child on that day, saying, 'It is because of what the LORD did for *me* when I came out from Egypt'." Therefore, it was not only our ancestors whom the Holy One, blessed is He, redeemed from slavery, *we were also redeemed together with them* (Babylonian Talmud, Tractate, "Pesachim," 116b).

We are celebrating on this night, in unity with the whole people of God, the great Passover sacrifice. "And when your children ask what does this service mean to you, you will answer that this is the Passover offering of the LORD who passed over the houses of the children of Israel in Egypt, when He struck Egypt" (Ex 12:27).

Father:

At the conclusion of our seder, we will join together in a simple Agape in memory of the fact that the Last Supper was the Passover observance at the time of the Temple. During the Passover supper, Jesus gathered all of us to himself in the ritual sharing at the breaking of bread (the Motzi-Matzah). After the supper, he joined us to himself in the new covenant of his love. Therefore, we will complete our evening, in unity with the whole family of God, with a rededication of ourselves to the new commandment of his Agape-Love (Jn 13:34,35).

The Passover seder is also the celebration of the love, compassion, and constant care that the Father of all mercy has for all of his children. Four times during the ritual, we are obligated to toast the LORD our God for our liberation from bondage. These four cups of the "Fruit of the Vine" are based upon the four promises that the LORD made to the children of Israel in Egypt through His servant, Moses:

וְהוֹצֵאתִ
"Wehotzeti"
"*And I will bring you out* from under the tribulations of Egypt."

וְהִצַּלְתִּי
"Wehitzalti"
"*And I will deliver you* from their slavery."

וְגָאַלְתִּי
"Wega'alti"
"*And I will redeem you* with an arm outstretched and with great judgments."

וְלָקַחְתִּי
"Welaqachti"
"*And I will take you* to Myself as My People."

וְהָיִיתִי
"Wehayiti"
"*And I will be* your God" (Ex 6:6,7).

Mother:

We read in the Mishnah that close to the hour of the evening sacrifice on the eve of Passover, a person must not eat anything until nightfall. Even the poorest in Israel must not eat anything until they are reclining at the Passover table. The hosts at each Passover supper should give to each person no less than four cups of wine. This is an obligation even if the food and drink must be supplied by money received from the charity plate (Babylonian Talmud, "Pesachim," Mishnah, 99b).[3]

At the time of the Second Temple, the wine was too strong or rough tasting to be drunk undiluted, since much of it was aged in pitch-lined animal hides. It was necessary to mix the wine with water to make it kosher for Passover. We read further in the Mishnah that these four cups must contain the standard mixture of water to wine, so that, as Rabbi Judah said, the mixture would still have the taste and appearance of wine. Furthermore, the rabbis taught that everyone was obligated to drink these four cups, including all of the women and children. Rabbi Judah is recorded to have rhetorically asked of what benefit is wine to women and children. It was decreed that they as well as the men were obligated to drink the four cups because women and children were also participants in that great miracle of the Exodus (Babylonian Talmud, "Pesachim," 108b).

1.
קַדֵּשׁ
Kaddesh
Sanctifying the Feast

Everyone has a glass set before them at table. The glasses are filled with wine or grape juice. Father first blesses the "Fruit of the Vine" and then he blesses the festival.[4]

The first cup is called the Kiddush Cup (כּוֹס שֶׁל קָדֵשׁ), the Cup of Sanctification.

Father holds up his glass to recite the blessing of the "Fruit of the Vine":

Blessed are you, O LORD our God,
the king of the universe
and creator of the Fruit of the Vine.

Father then recites the blessing for the festival:

We praise you, O LORD our God,
the king of the universe,
because you have chosen us
from among all the people of the earth,
and you have exalted us
from among those of every spoken tongue,
and you have sanctified us
through the observance of your
commandments.

Out of your love, you have given us seasons for gladness, holy festivals, and times for rejoicing.

You have given us this holy feast of unleavened bread, which we celebrate each spring as this was the season of our deliverance. This is a sacred assembly that calls us together in a memorial of our coming forth from Egypt.

Because you have chosen us and blessed us from among all the people of the earth, we have inherited this holy festival to celebrate in gladness and in joy. Therefore, we bless you, O LORD. And you bless Israel (the people of God) and the festival seasons.

Father concludes the Kiddush with the ancient blessing for all festivals:

We bless you, O LORD our God,
because you give to us our life.
You watch over us and you sustain us,
and you have brought us to this holy season.[5]

Everyone lifts up their wine or juice glass and recites the blessing:

Blessed are you, O LORD our God,
the king of the universe
and creator of the Fruit of the Vine.

Everyone now drinks their wine or juice. The glass should be emptied, but remember, there are three more glasses required in the ritual.

2.
וּרְחַץ
Urechatz
Washing of Hands

Father and Mother now rise, pick up the bowls and towels, and assist everyone with the first washing of their hands. There is no blessing recited for this first washing. The commandment stipulates that the hands must be washed before touching any food.

This first washing of the hands is a reminder that at the time of the Second Temple the men, women and children had to immerse themselves completely in the ritual bath before they could participate in the Passover feast.

After assisting everyone with the washing of their hands, Father and Mother return to their places and resume the seder service.

Reflection on the Washing of Hands: A Christian Addition

Since this would have been the time Jesus washed the disciples' feet, the following is included as a Christian addition to the traditional seder.

Reader:

Jesus, knowing that all things had been given to him by the Father, and that he had come forth from God and was now returning to God, rises from the supper and lays aside his outer garment, the Tallit. He takes a towel, and he girds it about himself. Then he pours water into a basin and he begins to wash the disciples' feet and to dry them with the towel which he has wrapped around him.

He then comes to Simon Peter who says to him, "Lord, are you going to wash my feet?" Jesus answers him, "What I am doing for you, you do not understand now, but you will understand me later.

Peter says to him, "You will not wash my feet—ever!"

Jesus answers him, "If I do not wash you, you have no place with me!"

Simon Peter says to him, "Lord, not only my feet but my hands and my head also."

Jesus says to him, "Having been bathed *(in the ritual bath)* there is no need but for the feet to be washed and you are all clean, but not all of you."

For he knew who would betray him and because of this he said, "Not all of you are clean." After he had washed their feet, he put on his outer garment and reclined again. He said to them,

Everyone:

"Do you understand what I have done for you?

You call me teacher and LORD, and you are correct, because I am.

If therefore I, the LORD and teacher, wash your feet—you also ought to wash one another's feet.

For I have given you an example: That as I did for you, you should do for each other.

As no slave is greater than his master, nor is a messenger greater than the one sending him.

If you understand these things, then you are blessed if you do them" (Jn 13:4-17).

3.

כַּרְפַּס

Karpas

Eating the Greens

This ceremony celebrates the arrival of spring as the season of our deliverance (Ex 13:4; "Abib," now pronounced "Aviv," means "spring").

The Karpas was the first course of the Passover supper at the time of the Second Temple. During this course, the roasted giblets of the paschal lambs were served on beds of leaf lettuce arranged upon large platters. It was the hors d'oeuvre before the main course of the meal. Pieces of lettuce were wrapped around the giblets and then they were dipped into bowls of saltwater or vinegar before they were eaten.

Today, parsley, watercress, celery or plain lettuce have replaced the giblets of Temple times. Everyone has a sprig of parsley on their plates. We will pick up these sprigs and dip them into the bowls of saltwater in the center of the tables. The saltwater represents the tears shed by the children of Israel while they were enslaved in Egypt.

Everyone says in unison:

Blessed are you, O LORD our God,
the king of the universe,
and the creator of the Fruit of the Earth.

Everyone dips their parsley sprigs into the salt water and eats them.

4.

יַחַץ

Yachatz

Breaking the Middle Matzah

One loaf of bread is served at the traditional Jewish meal. Two loaves, however, are served at the Sabbath supper on Friday evening as a reminder of the double portion of manna that was gathered each Friday by the Israelites in the wilderness (Ex 16:22). Because Passover is the preeminent feast of the Bible, three Matzot "loaves" are blessed and shared at the Passover supper.

The uppermost Matzah is named for the priest and is called "Kohen." The middle Matzah is named for the Levites and is called "Levi." The third Matzah is named for the people of God and is called "Yisrael."

These three "loaves" represent the three hereditary classes of the Jewish people at the time of the Second Temple. By everyone sharing them at the supper, they represent the unity of all the people at Passover.

Father removes the three Matzot from their protective cover and places then on a plate. He then breaks the middle Matzah in half, returns the two halves to the plate, and then up lifts the plate for all to see.

Father and Mother:

Behold this, the bread of affliction that our
ancestors ate in the land of Egypt!
Let all who are hungry come and eat with us,
let all who are needy come and share in our
Passover supper.
Now we are here, next year may we be in the land
of Israel!
Now we are slaves, next year may we all be free![6]

הָא לַחְמָא עַנְיָא דִּי אֲכָלוּ אַבְהָתָנָא
בְּאַרְעָא דְמִצְרָיִם.
כָּל דִּכְפִין יֵיתֵי וְיֵיכֺל / כָּל דִּצְרִיךְ יֵיתֵי וְיִפְסַח..
הָשַּׁתָּא הָכָא / לַשָּׁנָה הַבָּאָה בְּאַרְעָא דְיִשְׂרָאֵל .
הָשַּׁתָּא עַבְדֵי / לַשָּׁנָה הַבָּאָה בְּנֵי חוֹרִין .

It is the custom among many to turn on the porchlight at this point and leave the front door ajar for any unexpected guests. In the memory of past persecutions, others wait for the invitation of the prophet Elijah.

The Afikoman

The larger half of the broken Matzah is wrapped in a white napkin. This symbolizes the Israelites wrapping their unleavened dough in their bread troughs as they fled Egypt. This wrapped half of Matzah is reserved for the Afikoman to be eaten at the end of the meal. The seder ritual cannot be concluded without it. Father asks the children to cover their eyes while he hides it. The children, of course, will find the Afikoman and force Father to pay them something before they will give it back to him.

The smaller half of the broken Matzah will then be shared with the upper Matzah at the Ha-Motzi, which is the blessing of the bread that begins the formal meal.

The two other Matzot of the priest and the Levite are returned to their pockets in the Matzah cover.

The wine and juice glasses are now filled for the second time. This second cup is called the Cup of Narration (כּוֹס שֶׁל מַגִּד), Kos Shel Maggid.

The Afikoman:
A Christian Adaptation

The plate is returned to the table. Father wraps together both halves of middle Matzah in a white cloth and returns them to the Matzah cover or hides them in a safe place. Since the second Matzah could also represent the Son, the breaking, enshrouding, "burying," and then searching for it later could easily represent the death, burial, and resurrection of Jesus.

5.

מַגִּד

Maggid

Narrating the Exodus

The lengthy recital of the events of the Exodus begins with the traditional Four Questions. These questions are traditionally asked by the youngest child present or by the youngest person at the seder table. The Four Questions are customarily sung in Hebrew.

אַרְבַּע הַקֻשְׁיוֹת

The Four Questions

מַה נִּשְׁתַּנָּה הַלַּיְלָה הַזֶּה מִכָּל־הַלֵּילוֹת?

Mah NeeshtahNAH HaLEIGHlah Hazay MeeCOAL HalayLOAT?

Why is this night different from all other nights?

1. א. שֶׁבְּכָל הַלֵּילוֹת אָנוּ אוֹכְלִין חָמֵץ וּמַצָּה/
הַלַּיְלָה הַזֶּה כֻּלּוֹ מַצָּה.

ShehbuhKHOAL HalayLOAT Anoo OkhLEEN Chametz OO-Matzah.
HaLEIGHlah Hazeh Koolow Matzah.

On all other nights, we eat leavened or unleavened bread.
On this night we eat only unleavened bread.

2. ב. שֶׁבְּכָל הַלֵּילוֹת אָנוּ אוֹכְלִין שְׁאָר יְרָקוֹת/
הַלַּיְלָה הַזֶּה מָרוֹר.

ShehbuKHOAL HalayLOAT Anoo OkhLEEN ShehARE YehrahKOAT.
HahLEIGHlah Hazeh MaROAR.

On all other nights we eat all kinds of herbs.
On this night we eat bitter herbs.

3. ג. שֶׁבְּכָל הַלֵּילוֹת אֵין אָנוּ מַטְבִּילִין אֲפִילוּ פַּעַם אֶחָת/
הַלַּיְלָה הַזֶּה שְׁתֵּי פְעָמִים.

ShehbuKHOAL HalayLOAT Ayn Anoo MahtbeeLEEN AhFEEloo PahAHM ehKHAT.
HahLEIGHlah Hazeh ShTAY FayahMEEM.

On all other nights we don't dip even once.
On this night we dip twice.

4. ד. שֶׁבְּכָל הַלֵּילוֹת אָנוּ אוֹכְלִין בֵּין יוֹשְׁבִין וּבֵין מְסֻבִּין/
הַלַּיְלָה הַזֶּה כֻּלָּנוּ מְסֻבִּין.

ShehbuKHOAL HalayLOAT Anoo OkhLEEN Bayn YoshVEEN oo-Vayn MehsooBEEN.
HahLEIGHlah Hazeh KooLAHnoo Mehsoobeen.

On all other nights we eat either seated or reclining.
On this night we eat reclining.[7]

Father must now answer the young person's questions:

This night is very different from all other nights and you are very wise to ask us the reason for that difference. On this night, we will celebrate our Exodus from Egypt. Notice the table before us! It is especially set as the stage around which each one of us will participate in reliving that momentous event. Tonight, we will experience the flight from slavery to freedom; how the Almighty changed our sorrow to joy, and how the Holy One, Blessed is He, rescued slaves groveling in misery within the house of bondage and changed us through the observance of His commandments into His own liberated people, the people of God!

We eat only unleavened bread tonight because there was no time in our rush to freedom to allow our bread dough to rise.

> And the Egyptians pressured the people to hasten them while sending them away from their land; for they said, "All of us will be dead!" So the people took up their dough before it was leavened, binding their kneading troughs in their clothes and placing them upon their shoulders (Ex 12:33).

Mother:

We eat especially Bitter Herbs tonight to taste again the bitterness of slavery. As we read in the Torah,

> Egypt made the children of Israel to slave oppressively by making their lives *bitter* with hard work fashioning clay bricks and with all kinds of work in the field (Ex 1:13).

We dip our food twice this evening, once into saltwater to recall the tears shed in cruel slavery and bitter bondage, and we dip the harsh-tasting horseradish into the sweet Charoset to remind us to keep our faith in God, because He changes our cries of sorrow into shouts of joy.

Father:

We recline about the table this evening to recall that while the Holy Temple stood in Jerusalem, everyone reclined on couches at the Passover supper to express their joy of being set free on this night. As we read in Scripture,

> You shall tell your child, We were slaves to the Pharaoh in Egypt, but the LORD brought us out of Egypt with a powerful hand and by an outstretched arm" (Dt 6:21; 26:8).

If the Holy One, Blessed is He, had not brought our ancestors out of Egypt, then we and our children and our children's children would still be slaves to a Pharaoh in Egypt. Therefore, if we possessed all wisdom, and all understanding, and we were endowed with the wisdom of great age, and had complete understanding of the Sacred Scriptures, it would still be commanded of us to recount the events of our departure from Egypt. And whoever recalls the most details about our Exodus from Egypt is the most worthy of all our praise!

Mother:

An example of the meritorious discussion of the Exodus event is contained in the traditional Haggadah. It concerns some famous second-century rabbis at the school in Bene Berak, near ancient Jaffa. They were laboriously involved in writing down all of the previously memorized Oral Torah and the Oral Traditions of Temple times. Their completed written work became the Mishnah, the oldest part of the Talmud.

On this occasion, the learned rabbis were so engrossed in their analysis of the Exodus event that they lost all sense of time.

Father:

It happened at that time that Rabbi Eliezer, Rabbi Joshua, Rabbi Elazar ben Azariah, Rabbi Akiba and Rabbi Tarfon, as they were reclining about the seder table at Bene Berak while discussing the events of the Exodus from Egypt, they did not notice that they had been engaged in their deliberation all night long. Finally, their disciples came to them and said, "Our Masters, it is now time to recite the Morning Shema!"

Mother:

Rabbi Jose, the Galilean, said: "Since you say that the Egyptians in Egypt were beaten with Ten Plagues, then at the Red Sea they were stricken with fifty plagues! Why? What does it say (in the Bible) about the Egyptians? And the magicians said to Pharaoh, 'It is the *finger* of God' (Ex 8:15). But at the Red Sea, what does it say? 'And Israel saw the *Great Hand* with which the LORD acted against Egypt. The people were fearful of the LORD, and they had confidence in the LORD and Moses his servant' (Ex 14:31). By how much were they stricken by one finger? With Ten Plagues! Therefore, if it can be said that they were beaten by Ten Plagues in Egypt, then it follows that they were struck by fifty plagues at the Sea!"

Everyone:

Rabbi Elazar ben Azariah said, "Look, I am nearly seventy years of age and I could not recall why the Exodus from Egypt was discussed at night. Then Ben Zoma interpreted the verse in Scripture, 'As it is said, So that you may remember the day you came out of the land of Egypt *all the days of your life*' (Dt 16:3). '*Days of your life*,' he said, 'would mean only the days, but *all of the days of your life* means the nights as well!' Other Wise Men have said, '*days of your life*' means in this age only, but '*all of the days of your life*' means in the Messianic Age as well."

Father:

Blessed is our Omnipresent God, Blessed is He who gave the Covenant to His People Israel, Blessed is He!

Four times we read in Scripture that parents are commanded to explain the Passover ritual to their children:

> When your children shall say to you "what does this ritual mean to you" (Ex 12:26).

And you shall explain to you child on that day, saying, "This is because of what the LORD did for me when I came out from Egypt" (Ex 13:8).

When your child asks you, hereafter, "what does all this mean?" (Ex 13:14).

And when your child asks you in the future, "What are the testimonies, regulations, and laws that the LORD has commanded you to obey?" (Dt 6:20).

Mother:

From these verses, it is understood that the bible speaks to us about four different children: the Child who is Wise, the Rebellious Child, the Unsophisticated Child, and the Child who is too young to ask questions.

Father:

The Wise Child is attentive and asks, "What are the testimonies, regulations, and laws the LORD has commanded you to obey?" (Dt 6:20). You must instruct these children in the ancient customs and rules governing the observance of Passover. Introduce them into the ritual whereby we celebrate these obligations that are placed upon us. Especially the commitment that there is to be no eating nor involvement in any revelry after the Afikoman (Babylonian Talmud, "Pesachim," 119b).

The Rebellious Child says, "What does this ritual mean to you?" (Ex 12:26). Not feeling a part of the celebration, that child asks "to you" as an outsider having no place in the observance. That child should be answered, "This is because of what the LORD did for *me* when *I* came out from Egypt" (Ex 13:8). "For *me*" because I have accepted God's call to redemption, but that child would have remained a slave in Egypt by rebelling against God's actions in saving His people.

Mother:

The Unsophisticated Child asks, "What does all this mean?" and you will explain to that child, "By the might of his hand, the LORD brought us out of Egypt, out from the house of slavery" (Ex 13:14).

For the Child too young to ask why this evening is so different from all others, that child should be introduced to the story of the Exodus by interpreting the unusual items on the seder table and explaining in understandable language, "This is because of what the LORD did for *me* when *I* came out of Egypt" (Ex 13:8).

Everyone:

We read in the Mishnah that it is the duty of parents to instruct their children according to their intelligence. Parents are to begin the narration by explaining the shame experienced in slavery at the beginning and conclude the instructions by praising God for the deliverance of His people from oppression.

Father:

In the beginning, our ancestors worshiped idols, but our Omnipresent God called us to serve Him, as it says in Torah:

> And Joshua said to all the People, "Thus speaks the LORD (YHWH), the GOD of Israel, In the past, Terah the father of Abraham and the father of Nahor, your ancestors, lived beyond the river (Euphrates) and they served other gods. But I took your father Abraham from beyond the River and led him throughout all of the Land of Canaan. I multiplied his seed and give Isaac to him. To Isaac I gave Jacob and Esau. I gave the mountain region of Seir to Esau as his possession, but Jacob and his family went down into Egypt" (Jos 24:2-4).

Mother:

We bless the LORD who keeps His promise to Israel. For the Holy One, blessed is He, calculated the time He had allotted until He would fulfill His promise to our father Abraham, a promise He had made to him in the covenant cut between the animals' two halves (Gen 15:7-12). As we read,

> And He said to Abram: "You must know for certain that your descendants will become aliens in a land that is not theirs, and they will be enslaved and afflicted there for four hundred years. But, I will bring judgment against the nation that enslaves them and thereafter they will go out from it with great wealth" (Gen 15:13,14).

Everyone lifts up their glasses and says:

This promise made by God to our father Abraham was cherished by our ancestors, and it has sustained us as well. Because not just one person has risen up to destroy us, but in every succeeding generation another has appeared and attempted to exterminate us. But the Holy One, blessed is He, has always delivered us from out of their hands.

Everyone returns their glasses to the table.

Midrash on Deuteronomy 26:5[8]

Father:

It is wise to ask what the Aramean (Syrian) Laban intended to do to our ancestor, Jacob. While Pharaoh decreed that all newborn male infants should be killed, Laban wanted to exterminate Jacob and his whole family.

As we read in Scripture,

> An Aramean would have destroyed my father, but he went down to Egypt to live there with only a few people. And he became a nation there that was great and mighty and numerous (Dt 26:5)[9]

"He went down to Egypt" — Compelled by the will of God! (Gen 15:13,14).

"And he lived there" — Scripture teaches us that our ancestor Jacob did not go down into Egypt to settle, but only to sojourn there:

> And they said to Pharaoh, "We have come to sojourn in the land, because there is no grazing ground for your servants' flocks, as the famine is heavy in the land of Canaan. Now, please let your servants live in the land of Goshen" (Gen 47:4).

"Only a few people" — As it says,

> "Your ancestors went down to Egypt, just seventy people. But now the LORD (YHWH) your God has made you as numerous as the stars in the heavens" (Dt 10:22).

"He became a nation there" — We learn from this that Israel became a distinguishable group there (Ex 1:8,9).

"Great and mighty" — As it says in Scripture,

> And the children of Israel were fruitful and teeming and numerous, and became very, very strong. The land was filled with them (Ex 1:7).

"and numerous" — As it says,

> I have caused you to multiply like the shoots of the field. And you did multiply and become great and you became precious jewels. Your breasts have formed and your hair has grown, yet you are naked and bare (Ez 16:7).[10]

עֶשֶׂר מַכּוֹת
The Ten Plagues

Father:

These are the Ten Plagues with which God punished the Egyptians with ever-increasing intensity.

Everyone:

These are the Ten Plagues that fell upon the Egyptians because of their Pharaoh's stubborn arrogance!

Mother:

But all people are the children of our God. Even when they intend to destroy us, we cannot rejoice in their suffering. In the true spirit of the Haggadah, we must not rejoice in the suffering of others.

> "Is there not One Father of us all? Has not the One God created all of us? Why, then do we betray our brothers and sisters and thereby profane the Covenant of our Ancestors" (Mal 2:10).

The Egyptian people were severely punished because of their Pharaoh's hard-hearted refusal to release the Israelites from their bondage to him. But we cannot rejoice in their suffering, "Are you not like the children of the Ethiopians to me, O children of Israel?" Therefore, our second glass of wine cannot be full as we remember their torment. Instead, we will remove some of the wine or juice from our glasses.

Father:

So that our second cup, the Cup of the Exodus Narration, will not remain full, we will remove some of the "Fruit of the Vine." With a spoon or our little finger we will take some of the contents out of our glasses and drop it onto our plates as we name each one of the Ten Plagues:

Blood, "Dam" דם

Frogs, "Tzefardea" צְפַרְדֵּעַ

Lice, "Kinnim" כִּנִּים

Wild Beasts, "Awerove" עָרוֹב

Cattle Disease, "Dayver" דֶּבֶר

Boils "Shicheen" שְׁחִין

Hail "Barahd" בָּרָד

Locusts, "Arbeh" אַרְבֶּה

Darkness, "Choshekh" חֹשֶׁךְ

Death of Their Firstborn, "Makat Bekhorot"
מַכַּת בְּכֹרוֹת

Everyone:

We grieve over the horrors suffered by our fellow human beings so that we could be liberated. And yet, we can thank and we do praise our Lord and God for our redemption.

Everyone lifts their glasses and recites together:

And she, the Shekhinah [the cloud of fire and divine presence; Ex 13:21-22; 14:19-20], protected our forbearers and us. Not one enemy alone has risen up to destroy us, but rather, in every generation there have arisen individuals and groups intent upon annihilating us. But the Holy One, blessed is He, delivers us from their evil plans.[11]

Everyone sets their glasses down on the table.

Mother:

The mood of the narration suddenly changes at this point from the dwelling upon misery and suffering in

Egypt to the joy and happiness expressed by a free people living in their own land. The bridge to the next section is the delightful song, the "Dayyenu."

Father:

The Dayyenu has fifteen short verses that end with the one word chorus, "Dayyenu!" It is a Hebrew word that may be loosely translated as, "That alone would have been enough for us!" The fifteen verses are said to represent the number of steps from the Court of the Women in the Temple to the inner Court of the Priests. The Levites stood upon these steps during the Passover sacrifice and repeatedly sang the Hallel. "Hallel" is the Hebrew name for the collection of The Great Psalms of Praise (Ps 113-118; 136). "Halleluyah" means, "Let us sing The Great Psalms of Praise to YAH (YHWH)!"

Mother:

The Dayyenu also expresses the joy of the millions of pilgrims who ascended to Jerusalem each year for the feast of Passover while the Temple stood. There they actively participated in the Passover sacrifice in the Holy Temple. They came dressed in white because they all were elevated to the status of the priesthood for the pilgrimage feast of Passover ("Chag Ha-Pesach"), and were therefore required to wear the white linen robes and turbans of the clergy (Ex 39:27). As a memorial of the Passover sacrifice and universal priesthood of the people in Temple times, the tradition continues to this day of the men wearing white "Kipot" ("Yarmulkes") at the seder. Moreover, in observant Jewish homes, Father as Host wears a white garment as he leads his family in the Passover ritual.

Father:

Let us joyfully ascend to Jerusalem as well to participate in our memorial of the Passover sacrifice. That unique sacrifice was offered in the Holy Temple by Israelites[12] who had traveled from the ends of the known world to participate in this great paschal offering as "one people" (עַם אֶחָד). We will also participate in the paschal supper that was shared by all in the holy city of Jerusalem as a "single family" (מִשְׁפָּחָה אַחַת) by our sampling the symbolic foods of Temple times.

דַּיֵּנוּ
Dayyenu[13]

Everyone:

How many great blessings has the omnipresent Lord bestowed upon us?

Mother and Father:

If only He had brought us out of Egypt,
And not brought judgments upon them!

Everyone:

Dayyenu!

Mother and Father:

If only He had brought judgments upon them
And not defeated their gods!

Everyone:

Dayyenu!

Mother and Father:

If only He had defeated their gods,
And not slain their firstborn!

Everyone:

Dayyenu!

Mother and Father:

If only He had slain their firstborn,
And not given us their wealth!

Everyone:

Dayyenu!

Mother and Father:

If only He had given us their wealth,
And not divided the sea for us!

Everyone:

Dayyenu!

Mother and Father:

If only He had divided the sea for us,
And not made our way through the midst of it on dry land!

Everyone:

Dayyenu!

Mother and Father:

If only He had made our passage on dry land,
And not drowned our oppressors in the depths of the sea!

Everyone:

Dayyenu!

Mother and Father:

If only He had left our oppressors in the depths of the sea,
And not taken good care of us for forty years!

Everyone:

Dayyenu!

Mother and Father:

If only He had watched over us for forty years,
And not fed us with manna!

Everyone:

Dayyenu!

Mother and Father:

If only He had fed us with manna,
And not given to us the Sabbath!

Everyone:

Dayyenu!

Mother and Father:

If only He had given us the Sabbath,
And not brought us before the face of Mount Sinai!

Everyone:

Dayyenu!

Mother and Father:

If only He had brought us before Mount Sinai,
And not given the Torah to us!

Everyone:

Dayyenu!

Mother and Father:

If only He had given us Torah,
And not brought us into the Land of Israel!

Everyone:

Dayyenu!

Mother and Father:

If only He had brought us into the Land of Israel,
And not built for us His Holy Temple!

Everyone:

Dayyenu!

How much more then, in doubled and redoubled measure, has the Omnipresent One a claim upon our gratitude!

He brought us out of Egypt, and brought judgment upon them and upon their gods. He slew their firstborn and gave us their wealth! He divided the sea for us and led us through it on dry ground.

He plunged our oppressors into the depths of the sea!

He took care of us in the wilderness for forty years and He fed us with manna! He gave us the Sabbath for rest and He brought us before Mount Sinai, and He gave us the Torah!

He brought us into the Land of Israel and built for us His Holy Temple where we could atone for all our sins!

Mother:

The Passover supper of Temple times was the sacred banquet that completed the Passover sacrifice. Men, women, and children were all elevated to the dignity of the priesthood in order to participate. Therefore they came under the Levitical law of purification that required them to bathe in the ritual bath and put on white linen robes (Babylonian Talmud, "Pesachim," 109a,b). They then were privileged to eat the entire paschal lamb (Ex 12:8-10), not just the laity's portion (Lv 7:33-36). They all participated in the whole

Passover sacrifice, as well, because they all shared in the eating of the roasted flesh of the paschal offering that was the main course of the Passover supper.[14]

Father:

While the Temple stood, the great Rabbi Gamaliel used to say that whoever does not explain these three essential items at the Passover supper does not fulfill his paschal obligations (Babylonian Talmud, "Pesachim," Mishnah 116a,b).

And these three things are:

The Passover Sacrifice, "Pesach" פֶּסַח

The Unleavened Bread, "Matzah" מַצָּה

The Bitter Herbs, "Maror" מָרוֹר

Mother:

By emphasizing the equality of these three items, the rabbis were able to continue the observance of Passover without the sacrifice of the paschal lambs in the Temple and without the annual pilgrimage to Jerusalem where the paschal supper was eaten. By showing the unity of the one-day feast of Passover (Josephus, *Antiquities* [248]) with the seven-day Feast of Unleavened Bread (Josephus, *Antiquities* [249]), the unleavened bread was able to take the place of the paschal lamb as the sacrificial object to be shared in the seder supper.[15]

Everyone:

The roasted flesh of the Passover sacrifice that our ancestors ate at the time of the Temple, why was there the obligation to eat it?

Father:[16]

Because the Holy One, Blessed is He, *passed over* the houses of our ancestors in Egypt. As we read in Torah,

> It is the Passover sacrifice of the LORD (YHWH) Who passed over the houses of the children of Israel in Egypt, when He struck Egypt and spared our houses. And the people bowed and worshiped, and the children of Israel went out and did as the LORD (YHWH) had commanded Moses and Aaron (Ex 12:27,28).

Everyone:

This Matzah our ancestors ate, and which we eat on this night, what is the meaning of it?

Mother:

The women were required to make the unleavened bread very quickly because the dough our ancestors made had no time to rise when the King of kings revealed Himself to them and Redeemed them. As we read,

> And they baked the dough which they had brought out from Egypt into plain unleavened wafers, for it was not leavened; because they were driven out of Egypt and had no time to delay in order to prepare food for the journey (Ex 12:39).

Everyone:

These bitter herbs that our ancestors ate, and that we eat on this night, what is the reason for eating it?

Father and Mother:

Because the Egyptians made the lives of our ancestors bitter in slavery and, therefore, we must taste the same harshness as we share their bitter experience. As we read,

> And they made their lives bitter with hard work in clay and in the fashioning of bricks and with all kinds of work in the field. In all the work they

forced them to do, they pressured them with harshness! (Ex 1:14)

Father:

As we all share these three obligatory foods tonight, we are not simply remembering what happened so very long ago, we are actually participating in all of those events. This Passover ritual is called a "Zikaron" in Hebrew (Ex 12:14), an "Anamnesis" in Greek (1 Cor 11:24,25), and a "Memoriam" in Latin. The seder is a re-actualization of the Exodus. That means that by means of this Passover ritual we are not only bringing all of the events of the Exodus into the present so that we can also experience them, *it means that we actually become participants in all of events of the Exodus.*

Mother:

An undisputed commandment of the Oral Law from the time of the Temple is preserved in the Mishnah, and it says that *from generation to generation, each person is bound to regard himself or herself as personally coming forth out of Egypt.* As it says in the Torah,

> and you shall tell your child on that day that this is because of what the LORD (YHWH) did for me when I came out from Egypt" (Ex 13:8; Babylonian Talmud, "Pesachim" 116b).

Everyone lifts up their glasses and recites:

Therefore, it is our duty to thank, praise, laud, glorify, exalt, honor, bless, extol, and adore Him Who wrought all of these miracles for our ancestors and for ourselves.

He brought all of us forth from bondage into freedom, from sorrow into joy, from mourning into festivity, from darkness into great light, and from slavery into redemption.

Therefore, let us say before Him —
"Halleluyah!" (Babylonian Talmud,
"Pesachim," 116b).

The Hallel

The Hallel (Ps 113-118; 136) was chanted by the Levites in the Temple as the paschal lambs were sacrificed there. The Hallel was also sung by the people before and after eating their Passover supper. Psalms 113 and 114 were sung before the main course; Psalms 115 through 118 and Psalm 136 were sung after the blessing for the food. That was an obligation because it was a sacrificial meal. The Passover supper of Temple times was the conclusion of the Passover sacrifice. The Passover sacrifice was both a peace offering and communion sacrifice.

Everyone:

Halleluyah!

Praise Him, you servants of the LORD!
Praise the name of the LORD (YHWH)!

The name of the LORD (YHWH) is praised from
now and forever.
From the rising of the sun to its going down
the name of the LORD (YHWH) is praised.

The LORD (YHWH) is high above all the nations,
His glory above the heavens.

Who is like the LORD (YHWH) our God?
Who sits enthroned on high
and who looks down upon the heavens and the
earth.

He raises the poor up from the dust
and the needy from the dunghill
to sit them among the aristocracy
among the nobles of their own people

He causes the childless woman
to joyfully dwell in her house with her children.

Halleluyah!

Psalm 114

Everyone:

When Israel came out of Egypt,
the house of Jacob, from a people speaking an
alien tongue,

Mother and Father:

Judah became his sanctuary,
Israel his dominion.
The sea saw this and fled;
the Jordan river turned back!

Everyone:

The mountains skipped like rams,
the hills like lambs of the flock!

Mother and Father:

Sea, what is it that you flee?
Jordan, what is it that turns you back?
You mountains, why do you skip like rams?
You hills, like the lambs of the flock?

Everyone:

Before the face of the LORD
the earth trembles,
before the face of the God of Jacob!
Who turned the rock into a pool of water
and the flinty stone into a gushing spring.

Everyone lifts up their glasses and recites:

Blessed are you, O LORD our God,
the king of the universe,
our Redeemer and the Redeemer of our forbearers
in Egypt,
who brought us to this night on which we eat
unleavened bread and bitter herbs.
Therefore, O LORD our God and the God of our
ancestors,
bring us to other festivals and holy days that come
to us in peace,
joyful in the rebuilding of Your holy city and
joyous in Your service.
There we shall eat of the sacrifices and paschal
offerings whose blood will be worthily poured
out upon the sides of your altar.[17]

Everyone recites the blessing and drinks the second glass of the "Fruit of the Vine":

Blessed are you, O LORD our God,
the king of the universe,
and creator of the Fruit of the Vine.

6.
רַחַץ
Rachatz
The Second Washing of Hands

Mother:

We will now prepare to eat a little bit of the ritual food of Temple times. First, we must wash our hands for the second time before the Matzah is blessed and shared.

Mother and Father rise for the second time and, taking the bowls of water and towels, they assist everyone with the washing of their hands.

Everyone:

Blessed are you, O LORD our God,
the king of the universe,
You have sanctified us through the observance of
Your commandments,
and commanded us concerning the washing of our
hands.

7.
הַמּוֹצִיא
Ha-Motzi
The Breaking of Bread

After he returns to his place at the table, the Host of the seder, Father, just as was done at the time of the Temple, removes the top Matzah—the priests' loaf—from its safe place in the Matzah cover and recites the double blessing over it. The Matzah is first blessed as bread with the recital of the "Ha-Motzi," the traditional blessing of the bread said at the beginning of every Sabbath and holy day meal. Then the Matzah is blessed with its own blessing stating the requirement of eating only unleavened bread throughout the seven or eight days of Passover.[18]

Father, removing the upper Matzah from the Matzah cover, recites:

Blessed are you, O LORD our God,
the king of the universe
who brings forth bread from the earth.

בָּרוּךְ אַתָּה/ יְיָ אֱלֹהֵינוּ/ מֶלֶךְ הָעוֹלָם/ הַמּוֹצִיא לֶחֶם מִן הָאָרֶץ.

8.

מַצָּה

Matzah

Reciting the Blessing

Then, breaking the Matzah so that there is a piece for everyone, Father says:

Blessed are you, O LORD our God,
the king of the universe,
You have sanctified us through the observance of
Your commandments
and commanded us concerning the eating of this
Matzah.

בָּרוּךְ אַתָּה/ יְיָ אֱלֹהֵינוּ/ מֶלֶךְ הָעוֹם/
אֲשֶׁר קִדְּשָׁנוּ בְּמִצְוֹתָיו וְצִוָּנוּ עַל אֲכִילַת מַצָּה.

מוֹצִיא מַצָּה

Motzi-Matzah

Mother:

When everyone has received their piece of Matzah, take some of the salt on your plate and sprinkle it onto the Matzah. This reminds us of the sacramental nature of the Passover Matzah. It is salted just as the paschal lambs were salted as a sacrificial offering before roasting them over hot coals for the feast. Now, everyone will repeat the double blessing and eat the Passover Matzah.

Everyone:

Blessed are you, O LORD our God,
the king of the universe,
who brings forth bread from the earth.

Blessed are you, O LORD our God,
 the king of the universe,
You have sanctified us through the observance of
 Your commandments
and commanded us concerning the eating of the
 Passover Matzah.

9.

מָרוֹר

Maror

Eating the Bitter Herbs

Father:

We are now commanded to eat the bitter herbs. Because it is horseradish, this must be done carefully. With your spoon, take a very small portion of the Maror from your plate onto the spoon and then take twice as much of the Charoset onto the spoon as well—to cut the stinging effect that the horseradish has. When ready, we all will recite the appropriate blessing and eat the bitter herb.

Everyone:

Blessed are you, O LORD our God,
  the king of the universe,
You have sanctified us through the observance of
  Your commandments,
and commanded us concerning the eating of the
  bitter herbs.

10.
כּוֹרֵךְ
Korekh
Eating the Hillel Sandwich

Mother:

We will conclude our eating of a symbolic meal of Temple times by making the "Hillel Sandwich."

Father:

To the question put by a potential convert to Judaism, could Hillel recite the whole Torah while he was standing on one foot, the great sage responded by doing so while admonishing the young man, "Whatsoever is hateful to you, do not do to another! That is the whole Torah. All the rest is commentary!"

The Talmud records that Hillel used to wrap lamb and bitter herbs together in a soft Matzah. To Hillel, the commandment to eat the Passover lamb together with unleavened bread and bitter herbs (Ex 12:8) was an important obligation. Having a great understanding of the meaning of the Passover ritual, he realized that slavery and freedom were to be experienced together at the supper of the Passover sacrifice. The bread of affliction displayed at the invitation to Passover ("Ha-Lachma") was also the bread of freedom shared at the breaking of bread ("Ha-Motzi"). The Passover commentary teaches us that it is the obligation of free people to be ever mindful of those who are still bound in any kind of physical servitude, emotional bondage or political oppression. And all those still oppressed must never forget that our God is the God of liberation and of the liberators!

Mother:

Father will now remove the Matzah of the people, "Yisrael," from the Matzah cover. He will break it and divide it into enough pieces so that there are two pieces for everyone. Each one of us will make the Hillel Sandwich from them (Babylonian Talmud, "Pesachim," 115a).

Father:

Everyone take one of the pieces of the Matzah. Then place some of the bitter herb on it, along with some of the Charoset. Then close your Hillel Sandwich with the second piece of Matzah. Now let us all say together:

Everyone:

Blessed are you, O LORD our God,
the king of the universe,
You have sanctified us through the observance of
Your commandments
and commanded us to eat the paschal lamb
together with unleavened bread and bitter
herbs (Ex 12:8).

Everyone eats their Hillel Sandwich.

The Hillel Sandwich: A Christian Adaptation

Father:

The Passover Sacrifices ended when the Romans destroyed the Holy Temple; as a consequence, Jews can no longer eat the paschal lamb at their Passover suppers. The seder was then adapted by the rabbis in order to center the meal around the eating of unleavened bread as a substitute for the lamb eaten during Temple times. This was possible because the one-day feast of Passover had already become the first day of the seven-day feast of unleavened bread (Mk 14:1,12).

Mother:

But the Gospel of John (Jn 1:29,36) and the epistles of Paul (1 Cor 5:7) and Peter (1 Pt 1:19) saw in Jesus' death the final and perfect Passover sacrifice, which atones for all of our sins (Heb 9:11-28). In the second century, Melito of Sardis gave a Passover homily in which he explained how Christ had replaced the sacrifice of the Passover lambs in the Temple with his offering of himself. Justin Martyr continued the theme in his "Dialogue with Trypho." He considered the commandment to roast the whole lamb at Passover to be a symbol of Christ's death on the cross because the two wooden spits that transfixed the paschal sacrifice and held it over the fire actually formed a cross. Therefore, lamb holds a prominent place in a Christian seder.

Father removes the Matzah of the people, "Yisrael," from the Matzah cover. He breaks it, dividing it into enough pieces so that there are two pieces for everyone. Each one makes the Hillel Sandwich from these.

Father:

Everyone take one of the pieces of the Matzah. Then place some of the bitter herb on it, along with some of the Charoset. Then, removing the skewers from the piece of lamb, place the lamb morsel on the horseradish and Charoset. Close your Hillel Sandwich with the second piece of Matzah. Now let us all say together:

Everyone:

Blessed are you, O LORD our God,
the king of the universe,
You have sanctified us through the observance of
Your commandments
and commanded us to eat lamb with unleavened
bread and bitter herbs (Ex 12:8).

Everyone eats their Hillel Sandwich.

בֵּצָה

Baytzah

Eating the Roasted Egg: A Christian Addition

Mother:

Eating the Hillel Sandwich concludes the first part of the ritual of the Passover seder. However, there remains one more symbolic item on our seder plate. That is the roasted egg, called the "Baytzah." In Jewish homes, the roasted egg is eaten without any ceremony after it is dipped into salt water. It represents mourning for the loss of the Holy Temple and its sacrifices. But over the centuries Christians have taken this lowly egg and turned it into a joyous symbol of the resurrection.

Father:

After the destruction of the Temple by the Romans in 70 C.E. (A.D.) and the abolition of the Passover sacrifice there, paschal lambs could no longer be eaten by Jews at Passover. The rabbinical seder was created to enable the continuation of the Passover observance without the sacrificed lamb. The paschal lamb was replaced by the unleavened bread as the focal point of the service.

Mother:

But the Passover sacrifice and the Holy Temple were not forgotten. Upon the great platters that had once held the whole roasted paschal lambs during the Passover supper of Temple times, families now placed a roasted lamb bone in memory of the sacrificed Passover lamb and a roasted egg as a symbol of their mourning for the loss of the Temple. A hard-cooked egg had long been a token of mourning and an example of strength in adversity, because the longer it cooks the harder it gets.

Father:

The first Jewish Christians followed the same customs as their Jewish neighbors and relatives, because they mourned the loss of the Holy Temple as well. They soon realized, however, that Christians still had the ultimate Passover sacrifice, Jesus. As St. Paul wrote,

> Christ was sacrificed for us as our Passover! So that we should celebrate the feast, not with old leaven or the leaven of malice and wickedness, but with the unleavened bread of sincerity and truth! (1 Cor 5:7,8)

Mother:

Moreover, Christians were not bereft of the Temple as their Jewish kin were. As St. Paul also wrote,

> Do you not know that you are God's temple and the Spirit of God dwells within you? If anyone defile the temple of God, God will bring that person to ruin; because the temple of God is Holy, and that is what you are! (1 Cor 3:16,17)

Father:

Consequently, very early in the church, the Jewish emblem of mourning became the Christian symbol of the resurrection. The early Christians reasoned that just as the stony shell cannot contain the living chick within it and breaks when it hatches, the stone of the tomb could not restrain Christ when he rose from the dead.

Mother:

The custom arose in the Eastern church of smashing colored, hard-cooked eggs at Easter, while shouting, "Christ is risen," and then responding, "He is risen, indeed!"

Father:

To help us connect our Passover observance (פֶּסַח , "Pesach") with Easter, we must recognize that "Pascha" (in Greek, Πασχα) was the original name for Easter. That much we know from history, but what is not generally known is that the Greek word "Pascha" is actually the same word written in Greek letters as the Aramaic word for Passover, which is also (פִּסְחָא) or "Pascha!"

Let us all pick up our roasted egg and smash it onto our plates as we make our Easter and paschal proclamation.

Mother and Father:

Christ is risen!

Everyone smashes their eggs on their plate and responds:

He is risen indeed!

11.
שֻׁלְחָן עוֹרֵךְ
Shulchan Orekh
Dinner Is Served

The seder plate is now removed, and the table cleared for the dinner that has been prepared. The Passover ritual will conclude after dinner.

12.

צָפוּן

Tzafun

Returning the Afikoman

After dinner, the table is cleared of everything except the wine or juice glasses, the plate with the Matzah cover, the Elijah Cup, and the burning candles.

Father and Mother invite everyone to recover their Haggadahs for use during the remainder of the seder service. If he still has it, Father places the Afikoman (the "hidden" Matzah) on a plate before him and uncovers it for all to see.

If, however, the Afikoman has been spirited away and hidden somewhere by the children, Father must find out who has it and offer that child some reward for its return.

Since the Afikoman is the last thing to be eaten at the seder, the ritual cannot continue until the Afikoman is returned. Once returned, Father resumes the seder.[19]

This page corresponds to page **108** of *Celebrating an Authentic Passover Seder: A Haggadah for Home and Church* by Joseph M. Stallings (© 1994 Resource Publications, Inc.)

13.
בָּרֵךְ
Barekh
Giving Thanks for the Meal

Everyone's glasses are filled for the third time. In Hebrew, this third cup is called the Cup of Blessing (כּוֹס שֶׁל בְּרָכָה), or more familiarly, the Eucharistic Cup (1 Cor 10:16).

Father:

Let us say the blessing for our food, my honored friends.

Everyone:

The name of the Lord is praised from this time forth and forever!

Father and Mother:

Praised be our God of whose bounty we have partaken and through whose goodness we all live.

Everyone:

Praised is He and praised is His holy name.

Father:

Blessed are you, O LORD our God,
the king of the Universe,
Who, in Your goodness, sustain the whole world
with love, kindness, and compassion.
You provide food (bread) for all flesh (BaSaR),
for your mercy endures forever (Ps 136:25).

Because of your great love,
we have not lacked sustenance and may we never lack provisions for Your great name's sake.
You, O God, take care of all, do good to all, and provide food for all your creatures whom You have created.
Praised be You, O LORD, who provides food for all.

Mother:

We thank You, O LORD our God,
for the good, pleasant and spacious land which You have given to us as an inheritance from our ancestors,
for having liberated us from the land of Egypt, and redeemed us from the house of slavery.
We thank You for your covenant that You have sealed in our flesh,
for Your Torah which You have taught us, and for your Commandments which You have made known to us.
We also thank You for the gift of life which You, in Your love and kindness, have bestowed upon us,
and for the food with which You nourish and sustain us continually, in every season, every day, and even every hour.

Everyone:

For all these blessings, O LORD our God,
we give you thanks and we praise you.
May your holy name be praised by every living creature continually and forever,
as we are told in the Torah,
"and you shall eat and be satisfied, and you shall bless the LORD your God in the good land which He has given to you" (Dt 8:10).
We praise you, O LORD, for the land and its produce.

Father:

Have compassion, O LORD our God,
for Your People Israel,
for Jerusalem Your City,
for Zion the abode of Your Glory,
for the Royal House of David, Your Anointed,
and upon the great and Holy Temple called by
your Name.
Our God and our Father,
take care of and nourish us,
sustain and maintain us, and
speedily bring an end to all of our sorrows.

Everyone:

Our God and the God of our ancestors,
on this festival of unleavened bread,
be ever mindful of us and of our forbearers.
Hasten the age of the Messiah, the Son of David.
Remember Jerusalem your Holy City,
and all your people,
the House of Israel,
who are blessed by your deliverance, love,
kindness, mercy, life and peace!

Remember us on this day, O LORD our God,
to bless us with life and well-being.
With your promise of deliverance and mercy,
spare us and be gracious to us,
have compassion on us and save us.

We look to you, our God,
for you are a gracious and merciful king.

Father:

May the Merciful Father bless us and all who are
dear to us,
even as our fathers, Abraham, Isaac and Jacob
were blessed,
each with his own complete blessing;
May He bless each and everyone of us,
each of us with our own perfect blessing.

And to this let us all say...

Everyone:

Amen!

Everyone lifts up their glasses and recites:

Blessed are you, O LORD our God,
the king of the universe,
and creator of the fruit of the vine!

Everyone drinks their third glass, the Cup of Blessing, which was known to Greek-speaking Jews as the Eucharistic Cup.

14.
הַלֵּל
Hallel
Reciting the Hallel

All glasses are filled with the "Fruit of the Vine" for the fourth time. This fourth cup is called the Cup of the Hallel (כּוֹס שֶׁל הַלֵּל), "Kos Shell Hallel." At this time Father will also fill the Elijah Cup (כּוֹס שֶׁל אֵלִיָּהוּ), "Kos Shell Eliyahu." For many, it is customary at this time to open the door and turn on the porchlight as an invitation to the Prophet Elijah to join the family at the seder table.

Mother:

There is a universal belief that the prophet Elijah will appear at Passover and announce the arrival of the Messiah. That is why we open the door and pour a special cup of wine for him. Many believe that he enters every home at seder, and while not seen, he sips from the cup set out for him. Young children notice that after a little while there is less wine in his cup, especially if Father has drawn a line at the original level, and they are certain that Elijah did join them briefly.

Father:

The prophet Elijah is expected to explain the difficult sections of the Bible and to settle all disputes. He is predicted to bring peace and love to every family: "Behold, I am sending you the Prophet Elijah before the coming of the great and fearful Day of the LORD (YHWH), and he will turn the hearts of their parents to their children and the hearts of the children to their parents" (Mal 3:24). Let us greet the prophet with the ancient salutation offered to honored guests:

Everyone:

Blessed is he who comes!
(בָּרוּךְ הַבָּה) BaRUKH HaBAH!

Father and Mother:

Elijah, the Prophet,
Elijah, the Tishbite,
Elijah, the Gileadite!

Come speedily and bring
the Messiah, the Son of David!

Everyone:

Elijah, the Prophet,
Elijah, the Tishbite,
Elijah, the Gileadite!

Come speedily and bring
the Messiah, the Son of David!

הַלְלוּיָה
Halleluyah[20]

Psalm 115

Father:

Not to us, O LORD (YHWH), not to us,
but to your Name give glory,
because of your Love and your Truth.

Everyone:

Why do the Gentile nations say:
where is their God?

Mother:

Our God is in the Heavens
Finding pleasure in all that He has made.

Everyone:

Their idols are of silver and gold
they are the works of human hands.

They have mouths but do not speak
eyes that do not see
ears that do not hear
a nose but cannot smell.

Their hands cannot feel,
their feet cannot walk;
no utterance is heard in their throats.

Father:

Those who make them are like them,
Everyone who has faith in them!

Mother:

O Israel,
Have faith in the LORD (YHWH);
He is your helper and your shield.

O House of Aaron,
Have faith in the LORD;
He is your helper and your shield.

All you who revere the LORD
Trust in the LORD;
He is your helper and your shield.

Everyone:

The LORD is ever mindful of us;
He will bless us,
He will bless the house of Israel,
He will bless the house of Aaron,
He will bless all those who revere him
from the least to the greatest.

Father:

He will add to you
Add to you and your children.

Everyone:

Blessed are you O LORD (YHWH)
who made the heavens and the earth.

The heaven of heavens belong to the LORD
(YHWH)
but the earth He has given to the children of
Adam.
The dead do not praise the LORD
nor those who go down into the grave
but we will bless the LORD
from now and forever!

Halleluyah!

Psalm 116

Father:

I love,
because the LORD (YHWH) hears my voice
and my prayers.

Mother:

He inclined His ears to me.
Throughout my day
I will call upon Him.

Everyone:

But the cord of death encircled me
  and the boundaries of the grave overtook me.
I find myself in anguish and in grief.

Father:

I call upon the Name of the LORD (YHWH)
  I beseech You, O LORD (YHWH)
    Save my life!

Mother:

The LORD (YHWH) is compassionate and just.
Our God is merciful;
  the LORD (YHWH) protects the defenseless.

Everyone:

I was low
  but the LORD (YHWH) saved me.
Return O my life to your resting place
  because the LORD (YHWH) has rewarded you!

Father:

Having pulled my life out of death,
  my eyes away from tears,
  and my feet from stumbling.

Mother:

I will walk before the LORD (YHWH)
  in the land of the Living.
I have believed, therefore I speak!

Everyone:

Before I was greatly afflicted
  and I said in my alarm, "Everyone is a liar."

Father and Mother:

What shall I return to the LORD (YHWH)
for all that He has bestowed upon me?
I will lift up the Cup of Salvation
and I will call upon the Name of the LORD
(YHWH)!

Everyone:

Please now will I pay my vows to the LORD
(YHWH)
in the presence of all of His people!

Mother and Father:

Costly is the death of His faithful ones
in the eyes of the LORD (YHWH).
I pray, O LORD (YHWH), that I am truly your
servant.
I am your servant and the Child of your
Maidservant
and You have loosened my bonds.

Everyone:

I will sacrifice to you the sacrifice of thanksgiving
and I will call upon the name of the LORD
(YHWH)
I will pay my vows, please now! To the LORD
(YHWH)
in the presence of all of his people
in the courts of the house of the LORD (YHWH)
in the midst of you, O Jerusalem!

Halleluyah!

Psalm 117

Mother and Father:

Praise the LORD (YHWH) all you nations!
Praise Him all you peoples!

Everyone:

Because He is mighty over us
and the truth and the love of the LORD (YHWH)
are forever!

Halleluyah!

Psalm 118

Father and Mother:

Give thanks to the LORD (YHWH), for He is good,
His Love for us is forever!

Everyone:

Let the house of Aaron say,
that his love for us is forever!

Let the God-fearing say,
that His love for us is forever!

Father:

Out of my distress I called upon the LORD (YHWH)
And He answered me and set me free!

Mother:

The Lord is with me,
I will not be afraid.
What can anyone do to me?

Father:

The LORD is with me as my helper,
I shall see the downfall of my enemies.

Mother:

It is better to rely on the LORD
Than to depend upon any person.

Everyone:

It is better to rely upon the LORD
than to depend upon princes.

Many nations encircled me;
in the name of the LORD I overcame them!

They circled all about me;
in the name of the LORD I overcame them!

They swarmed about me like bees;
they were consumed as a fire among thorns
because in the name of the LORD I overcame them!

Father:

They thrust at me to make me fall;
but the LORD (YHWH) came to my assistance.
The LORD (YHWH) is my strength and my song,
and He has become my Deliverer.

Listen! The joyous song of victory
is heard in the tents of the Righteous;

The might of the LORD (YHWH) is triumphant!
The power of the LORD (YHWH) is exalted!
The strength of the LORD (YHWH) is victorious!

Mother:

I shall not die, but will live
to recount the works of the LORD.

The LORD has severely chastened me
but He has not given me over to death.

Open to me the Gates of Righteousness
that I may enter and praise the LORD.

This is the Gate of the LORD,
the Righteous alone shall enter here!

(By ancient tradition, each of the following verses is repeated:)

Father and Mother:

I thank You, O LORD,
that You have answered me,
and have become my Deliverer.
The stone that the builders rejected,
has become the cornerstone!
This is the work of the LORD,
and it is marvelous in our eyes!

Everyone:

I thank you, O LORD (YHWH),
that you have answered me,
and have become my deliverer.
The stone that the builders rejected,
has become the cornerstone!
This is the work of the LORD (YHWH),
and it is marvelous in our eyes!

Father and Mother:

This is the day which the LORD (YHWH) has
made;
Let us rejoice and be glad in it.

I beseech You, LORD (YHWH),
salvation please now ("Hoshiah Na"[21])!
I beseech You, LORD (YHWH), success please
now!

Blessed is He who comes in the Name of the LORD.
We bless Him from the House of the LORD!

Everyone:

This is the day which the LORD has made;
let us rejoice and be glad in it!

I beseech you, LORD (YHWH),
salvation please now ("Hoshiah Na")!
I beseech you, LORD (YHWH), success please now!

Blessed is He who comes in the Name of the LORD.
We bless Him from the House of the LORD!

Father and Mother:

God is LORD (YHWH) and He has given us light;
join the festival procession with woven branches
up to the horns of the Altar (singing),
"You are my God and I thank You!"
"You are my God and I extol You!"

Everyone:

God is LORD and He has given us light;
join the festival procession with woven branches
up to the horns of the altar (singing),
"You are my God and I thank you!"
"You are my God and I extol you!"

Father and Mother:

Give thanks to the LORD for He is good,
because His love is everlasting!

Everyone:

Give thanks to the LORD for He is good,
because His love is everlasting!

Prayer Concluding the Hallel

Everyone:

All your works praise you, O LORD our God,
and your faithful ones,
the just who do your will,
together with all your people,
the house of Israel,
shall praise you in joyous song.

We shall thank, exalt, revere and sanctify you,
and ascribe sovereignty to your holy name,
O our king!

For it is good to give you thanks and it is fitting to
sing praises to your holy name,
for you are God from everlasting unto
everlasting!

15.
נִרְצָה
Nirtzah
Conclusion of the Seder

Everyone:

Blessed are you, O LORD our God,
the king of the universe.
We praise you for the vine
and the fruit of the vine
and for the produce of the field,
for the broad, good and beautiful land
that you were pleased to bestow
upon our ancestors and upon us
that we may eat from its fruitfulness
and be satisfied by its goodness!
Please now!
Be compassionate with your people, Israel,
over your city, Jerusalem,
over Zion, the place of your glory,
and over your sanctuary.

We rejoice on this day
the feast of unleavened bread
because you are good
O LORD,
and the benefactor to all.
We thank you for the land
and for the fruit of the vine.

Blessed are you O LORD
for the land
and for the fruit of the vine!

Mother and Father:

Now our seder is concluded,
every law and custom fulfilled;

as we have gathered here to celebrate this Passover
tonight
may we be able to gather again for seder next year.

O pure one who dwells on high!
Raise up the countless assembled congregations of
your people,
and speedily lead the offshoots of your stock,
now redeemed,
to holy Zion with song!

Everyone:

Blessed are you, O LORD our God,
the king of the universe
and creator of the Fruit of the Vine.

Everyone drinks the Cup of the Hallel, then exclaims:

Next year in Jerusalem!

Notes

1. This prayer over the festival lights is ancient. It does not mention candles because at the time of Christ oil lamps were used. Oil lamps were lit by mothers and wives before all sabbaths and festivals, especially the Passover supper. Oil lamps at the time of the Second Temple were constructed to hold enough oil to burn from sunset to sunset. Jesus' mother said this prayer over the oil lamps in her home on all the sabbaths and holidays of her life and may very well have led the other women in this prayer before the Last Supper.

2. At the time of Christ, the bible or Torah was believed to have two parts. One was the Written Bible, but of equal importance was the Oral Teachings of the great sages. The Oral Teachings were not written down but were memorized by the disciples of the rabbis. There was a special class of disciple that was adept at memorizing. Called "Tanna'im," a Tanna was an authority on the Oral Torah and the Oral Teaching of the religious authorities. Only after the destruction of the Jewish nation by the Romans in 66-73 AD did the rabbis collect the memorized Oral Teaching in writing to preserve it.

3. Throughout history, Jewish communities have taken up collections to insure that every family has enough to eat and drink at Passover so that their seders are joyful. It is from that same sense of responsibility for the needs of others that we continue that tradition with our charitable collections of food and toys for the poor at Thanksgiving and Christmas.

4. Jesus certainly recited these two blessings at the Last Supper, since both are discussed in the Mishnah. Luke states that Jesus took the first cup at the beginning of the supper and blessed it by reciting the Kiddush, and then he said, "Take this and divide it among you" (Lk 22:17). Sharing the Kiddush Cup had special meaning at the time of the Second Temple. Because very great crowds assembled in Jerusalem at Passover, many families had to join together as a single group for the celebration. Yet Exodus 12:3 states the Passover lamb must be eaten by families, so using Exodus 12:4 as a rationale, several families were joined together as one family by sharing the one Kiddush Cup.

5. This blessing, called the "Shehecheyannu," was not said at the Last Supper. At the time of the Second Temple, this prayer was said by a priest over the firstborn son of a family when the child was "purchased back from the LORD" by his parents with a simple sacrifice in the Temple. The ceremony was called "pidyon haben" (Lk 2:22-24). After the Temple was destroyed and the Passover sacrifice could no longer be offered there, the rabbis decreed that the blood shed by the firstborn at his circumcision (the "B'rith Milah" or the "circumcision covenant") was a suitable substitution for the atoning blood of the Passover lambs shed during Temple times for the sanctification of the feast. The redeeming prayer over the firstborn was then added to the Passover supper ritual to express this later sanctification.

Subsequently, the Shehecheyanu was added to the Kiddush on the first day of all the festivals.

6. This prayer is usually recited in Aramaic instead of Hebrew. Aramaic is the language acquired by the Jews during their Babylonian captivity. Scholars are fairly unanimous in believing that this prayer originated in Babylon as well because the prayer suggests that the people are still enslaved and are exiled from the land of Israel. Even in Aramaic, which was the everyday language that Jesus spoke, there are several Hebrew names, such as "Mitzrayim" (Egypt), "Pesach" (Passover) and "Yisrael" (Israel).

7. This fourth question was not asked at the Last Supper. Instead the children asked, "On all other nights we eat meat roasted, stewed or boiled. On this night we eat only roasted meat." After the destruction of the Temple, no paschal lambs could be eaten at Passover, and then the question about boiled or roast meat was replaced by this one about reclining.

8. The traditional Haggadah is the source of this ancient Midrash on Deuteronomy 26:5.

9. The first line of Deuteronomy 26:5 should read "My father was a wandering Aramean." For the sake of this Midrash, however, the vowels of the Hebrew word,"oBeD" are changed to "iBeD," which means "would have destroyed." Scholars believe that this is a disguised reference to the Syrian king Antiochus IV Epiphanes, who intended to abolish Judaism.

10. Israel was youthful but still immature in Egypt. Maturity came with Israel's acceptance of the Covenant (Torah) at Mount Sinai. Deuteronomy 26:5-10 was a profession of faith made on the feast of Pentecost (Dt 26:1-11). At the Pentecost (Shavuoth) profession, the first line reads, "My father was a wandering Aramean." Many traditional Haggadahs contain a Midrash of all of Deuteronomy 26:5-10.

11. Karen G. R. Roekard, *The Santa Cruz Haggadah* (Capitola, California: Hineni Consciousness Press, 1991), 29.

12. "An Israelite killed the paschal lamb and the priest caught the animal's blood in a basin." Was a layman permitted to sacrifice? The Tanna informs us that was indeed the case! It is lawful that the ritual slaughter of the Passover sacrifice be done by a lay Israelite. "And the priest caught the blood" informs us that it became the obligation of the priest, from the time he received the blood in a basin until the blood was "sprinkled" against the sides of the altar (Babylonian Talmud, "Pesachim," 64b).

13. This song, or one very much like it, was sung at the Last Supper. It was and is very popular. Historians noted that since the refrains end with a reference to the Temple, the song existed at Second Temple times, if not long before.

14. Baruch M. Bokser, *Origins of the Seder*, Berkeley: University of California Press, 1984. It is recorded in the Mishnah that Rabbi Judah ben Bathyra taught that while the Second Temple existed, the rejoicing at the Passover supper must be centered upon the eating of the roasted flesh of the paschal lamb. The Hebrew word for "flesh" is "BaSar" and means "body," "flesh," "flesh of the sacrifice," and "living creature" or "person." The Aramaic word is almost identical, "BiSRA," and means exactly the same thing. Our Lord's words at the Last Supper were "DeN BiSReY": "This, My Body."

15. Josephus explained in *Antiquities of the Jews* that the feast of Passover was celebrated on the 14th of the Hebrew month Nisan (III, 10, 5.[248]) and the Feast of Unleavened Bread began on the 15th (III, 10, 5.[249]). Although all the people had to remain in Jerusalem throughout the 14th and 15th, they could leave on the 16th. If the Sabbath fell on the 15th or 16th, however, then the people could not leave until the 17th. The Priests and Levites, on the other hand, had the obligation of observing all seven of the succeeding days in the Temple, "for it is intended as a feast for the priest(s) on every one of those days."

16. Father reads this because the laymen did the actual sacrifice of the lambs in the Temple.

17. This blessing was added to the first part of the Hallel by the second-century Rabbi Akiba.

18. These two blessings were said by Jesus at the Last Supper. The Gospels state that during the meal Jesus took bread, blessed and broke it and gave it to his disciples (Mk 14:22). By their calling the Matzah "bread," they identify that this was at the Motzi-Matzah of the Passover supper, wherein the unleavened bread is first blessed as bread and then as Matzah. It is then broken and shared with everyone. The breaking and sharing of bread had great meaning for the Jews; called the Ha-Motzi, it signified that the sharing of bread and the meal united everyone in a special covenant relationship. Naturally, the original name for the Eucharist was "Ha-Motzi," the "Breaking of Bread" (Acts 2:42).

19. The Afikoman is traditionally eaten at this point. A Christian adaptation of the ritual reserves the Afikoman for the Agape observed after the conclusion of the seder.

20. Psalms 115, 116, and 117 may be omitted. For a shorter service turn to page 119.

21. The original meaning of "Hosanna," "Hoshiah Na," is "Salvation Please Now!" and not "Hurray." The crowds of people were not cheering Jesus upon his entry into Jerusalem; they were imploring him to liberate them from the cruel Romans.

AGAPE

A CHRISTIAN CONCLUSION TO THE SEDER

Father:

We will conclude our evening with a Christian adaptation of the Afikoman. In the Jewish home, the Afikoman is eaten just before the thanksgiving grace after the supper is recited. At the time of the Temple, when the paschal lambs were still sacrificed in the Temple and the roasted flesh eaten at the Passover suppers throughout the Holy City, the Afikoman was a piece of the sacrificed lamb "about the size of an olive" eaten in a formal Hillel Sandwich. That final morsel of the paschal lamb was combined with Matzah and Maror (Ex 12:8) and was eaten just before the prayer of affirmation was recited at the Nirtzah, concluding the Passover ritual. That ritual consumption of the flesh of the paschal lamb, while stating that all customs and laws had been fulfilled, was an affirmation that all paschal obligations had been met.

Mother:

Jesus gathered all of us to himself at the Motzi-Matzah, the breaking of bread, of that last Passover supper. In our respectful recognition of the Eucharist which he bequeathed to us, we will share the Afikoman of our seder in a simple ceremony expressing our Agape-Love.

Father:

In this simple Agape, we will also share the Elijah Cup. The Elijah Cup may be called the fifth cup of the Passover Supper. In Jewish homes it is filled with wine but never drunk from.

Mother:

When Jesus took a cup after the supper, whether it was the third, which was called the Eucharistic Cup, or the fifth, which we call the Elijah Cup, and announced to his disciples that it now contained "The Blood of the Covenant" (Mk 14:24), the disciples understood him.

Father:

The disciples were well versed in the fact that the children of Israel were sealed to the LORD God of Israel by "The Blood of the Covenant." When the covenant was to be ratified at Mount Sinai,

> Moses related to the people all the commanding words (commandments) of the LORD (YHWH) and all of the judgments. Then all of the people replied with one voice, saying "All of the commanding words that the LORD (YHWH) said, we will do!" (Ex 24:3).

Then Moses had twelve stone pillars set up to represent the twelve tribes and an altar built to represent God. Burnt offerings were made to God and bullocks were sacrificed as Peace offerings. Moses had the blood that was drained from the sacrifices placed in large basins. He took half of the blood and threw it upon the altar.

> He took the book of the covenant (commanding words) and read it to the listening people. And they said that "All that the LORD (YHWH) has said, we will hear and we will do." Then Moses took the remaining basins of blood and threw it onto all of the people, sealing them to God in the covenant. Moses announced, "Behold, the blood of the covenant which the LORD (YHWH) has cleaved Himself to you according to all of these commanding words" (Ex 24:8).

Mother:

Although the synoptic Gospels (Matthew, Mark and Luke) may seem to present a separate tradition from the fourth Gospel (John) concerning the origins of the Eucharist, the seemingly separate traditions are one. You cannot separate a covenant, whether it is the Sinai Covenant or the New Covenant (1 Cor 11:25) from its commandments. Moses had the Israelites vow obedience to the commandments before he sealed them to God with the blood covenant.

Consequently, the New Covenant proclaimed in the synoptics (Mt 26:28; Mk 14:24; Lk 22:20) and Paul (1 Cor 11:25) cannot be separated from the New Commandment found in the fourth Gospel (Jn 13:34,35):

I give to you a new commandment:
  that you should love one another,
  that you should love each other just as I have
    loved you!
By this shall everyone know that you are my
    disciples,
  if you love one another.

Father:

Therefore, we cannot say that we are faithful to the New Covenant of Christ if we ignore his new commandment. We must "love one another" as our brothers and sisters in Christ. We are the children of the one God.

Mother and Father:

As our Afikoman, we will all now share this one "loaf" that was hidden from us and then found by us again. We will simply express in this sharing of bread the Agape-Love that we have for one another.

> Although we are many individuals, because of the one bread we are one body by sharing the one bread (1 Cor 10:17).

At this final breaking of bread, this simple and plain unleavened bread becomes a symbol of the life we all share intimately together in the love of Christ.

Father takes the two halves of the Afikoman. Taking a small piece for himself to eat, he passes the two halves to those seated on either side of the table.

As the Agape-Afikoman is shared, Father reads the following:

But be eager for the better gifts (charismata)
and yet I will show you a more excellent way:

If I speak with the tongues of men and of the angels,
but do not have love (Agape)
I have become as brass sounding or a cymbal clanging!

And if I prophesy,
and if I know all the mysteries and possess all knowledge,
and if I have all the faith necessary to remove mountains,
but I do not have love (Agape)—
then I am nothing!

And if I give away all my goods to give food to the poor
and deliver up my body that I may be burned,
but I do not have love (Agape),
I have gained nothing!

Love has patience,
love is kind,
it is not envious.
Love is not boastful nor puffed up,
it is not indecent,
nor seeks things for itself.
It is not easily provoked
nor thinks evil of others.
It rejoices in truth,
it covers all things,
it believes in all things,
places its hope in all things,
and endures all things.

Love never fails:
prophesying shall be done away with,
speaking in tongues will cease,
knowledge will fail us.

For now, we only know in part,
and in part we prophesy.
But when the perfect state comes,
then what we know only in part
shall be done away with!

When I was a young child,
I spoke as a young child,
and thought as a young child.
But now that I am an adult
I have put behind me those things of childhood.
Now we see things as a riddle in a darkened mirror,
but then we shall see face to face!
I have only partial knowledge now,
but then I shall know, just as I am known!

Of all the things that we have now,
only these three will remain,
and they are faith, hope and love,
but the greatest of all of these is agape-love!
(1 Cor 13:1-13).

Mother:

Now we will all share the fifth cup of the seder, the Elijah Cup. We will all share the Elijah Cup in our simple Agape-Afikoman in respect for the new covenant into which Christ sealed us to himself and to each other with his own blood. For, just as Moses sealed the children of Israel to God at Mount Sinai, and to each other in a covenant relationship by pouring the blood of the covenant upon the altar of God and splashing the remaining onto the people (Ex 24:3-8), our Lord Jesus sealed us to himself and to each other in the new covenant relationship of the family of God by his own blood of the new covenant (1 Cor 11:25).

Father sips from the Elijah Cup and passes it to those around the table.

Father:

Beloved
let us love each other,
because love is of God
and everyone who loves
has been born of God
and knows God!

Anyone who is not a loving person
has never known God
because God is love.

The love of God was manifested to us in this way,
God sent his only begotten son into the world
that we might live through him!

In this love,
it is not that we have loved God,
but that he loves us so very much
and sent his son as the offering for our sins.

Beloved,
if God has loved us so much
we must also love each other.
For no one has ever seen God,
yet, if we love each other
God resides within us
and his love is perfected in us!

By this do we know that we reside in him
and he in us,
because of his spirit that he has given to us!

And we have seen and bear witness
that the Father has sent the Son
as the savior of the world.
Whoever confesses that Jesus is the Son of God
God resides in that person and that person in
God!

And we have known and have believed
in this love which God has for us.

God is love
and whoever remains in love
dwells in God,
and God dwells there within.

Love is perfected within us in this way,
that we have confidence on the day of judgment,
for even as he was
so we are also, in relation to this world.
There is no fear in love
because perfect love casts out fear.
Fear has to do with punishment
and love has not been made perfect in someone who fears!

We love him because he first loved us.
And if anyone should say that they love God
and yet hates a brother or sister,
that one is a liar!

For if someone does not love the brother or sister they see
how can they love God whom they cannot see?

The commandment that we have from him is this:
that by loving God, we also love our sisters and brothers! (1 Jn 4:7-21)

Peace and Blessing.

Pax et Bonum.

Paz y Bien.

Shalom u-Vrakhah.

Appendix

Pronouncing the Hebrew Prayers

The English transliteration of Hebrew—the writing of Hebrew using the English alphabet—is a common practice. It enable those who cannot read Hebrew to at least pronounce the Hebrew blessings.

Pronounce vowels as you might if your were speaking a Latin language (Spanish, Italian, etc.):

"a" is pronounced "ah" as in "father"

"e" (short) is pronounced "eh" as in "bell"
"e" (long) is pronounced "ay" as in "bay"

"i" is pronounced "ee" as in "machine"

"o" is pronounced "o" as in "go"

"u" is pronounced "oo" as in "blue"

Two vowel combinations must be carefully noted:

"ay" is pronounced like a long "i" as in "high"

"ey" is pronounced like a long "a" as in "bay"

In other vowel combinations, each vowel is pronounced separately. For example, "Israel" is pronounced "Yisra'el" (Yees-rah-ell).

All the consonants in Hebrew are pronounced like English consonants, including "y" as in "yellow." The "r" is properly pronounced as in Spanish or Italian, although in Israel one can hears it in conversation with a German, French, and Moroccan pronunciation.

The consonant combination "sh" is pronounced the same as in English. "Tz" is a little harder, pronounced "ts" as in "cats." Two others are usually quite difficult for Americans:

> "kh" is pronounced "ch" as in the German "ach" or Scottish "loch"
>
> "ch" is pronounced as the Spanish "j" as in "jota" or the Slavic "h."

In conversation, however, many Israelis pronounce "ch" the same as "kh" even though "ch" should be sounded in the throat and "kh" in the back of the mouth. If these two combinations are too difficult to master, pronounce both of them as the English "k."

After practicing these sounds for a while, try this sentence:

> Barukh ata Adonay, Elohenu, melekh ha olam.

It should sound like:

> Bah-rookh ahtah Ah-doe-Neigh, El-low-hay-noo, meh-lekh hah oh-lahm.

Now you are ready to try the seder blessings.

Lighting the Holy Day Lights (page 60):

> Barukh ata Adonay, Elohenu, melekh ha olam,
>
> (Blessed are you O LORD our God,
> the king of the universe,)
>
> Asher kidshanu bemitzvotav
>
> (that sanctified us by your commandments)

Vetzivanu lehadlik ner shel yom tov.

(and commanded us
to light the lights for the good day.)

Blessing the Fruit of the Vine (page 64):

Barukh ata Adonay, Elohenu, melekh ha olam,

(Blessed are you O LORD our God,
the king of the universe,)

Borey Pri ha Gafen.

(creator [of the] Fruit of the Vine.)

Blessing the Karpas (page 69):

Barukh ata Adonay, Elohenu, melekh ha olam,

(Blessed are you O LORD our God,
the king of the universe,)

Borey Pri ha Adamah.

(creator [of the] Fruit of the Earth.)

Invitation to Passover (page 70):

This invitation is actually spoken in Aramaic, the language Jesus spoke.

Ha lachma anya di akhalu avhatana

(Behold, the bread of poverty that was eaten by
our ancestors)

Be' arah de Mitzrayim.

(in the land of Egypt.)

Kol dikhfin yeytay veyekhol,

(All hungry come and eat,)

Kol ditzrik yaytay veyiFsach.

(All needy come and [join] our Passover.)

Hashatah hakhah, leshana haba'ah be arah
deYisra'el.

(Now we are here, in the year coming may we be in the land of Israel.)

Hashatah avdey, leshana haba'ah, beney chorin!

(Now we are slaves, in the year coming may we be free!)

Blessing the Bread, Ha-Motzi (pages 96, 97):

Barukh ata Adonay, Elohenu, melekh ha olam,

(Blessed are you O LORD our God,
the king of the universe,)

Ha motzi lechem min ha aretz.

(who brings forth bread from the earth.)

Blessing the Unleavened Bread (page 97, 98):

Barukh ata Adonay, Elohenu, melekh ha olam,

(Blessed are you O LORD our God,
the king of the universe,)

Asher kidshanu bemitzvotav

(that sanctified us by your commandments)

Vetzivanu al akhilot Matzah.

(and commanded us concerning the eating of unleavened bread.)

Blessing the Bitter Herb (page 99):

Barukh ata Adonay, Elohenu, melekh ha olam,

(Blessed are you O LORD our God,
the king of the universe,)

Asher kidshanu bemitzvotav

(that sanctified us by your commandments)

Vetzivanu al akhilot Maror.

(and commanded us concerning the eating of the bitter herb.)